Poetry Motion

Lothian
Edited by Chris Hallam

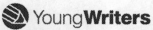 Young**Writers**

First published in Great Britain in 2004 by:
Young Writers
Remus House
Coltsfoot Drive
Peterborough
PE2 9JX
Telephone: 01733 890066
Website: www.youngwriters.co.uk

SB ISBN 1 84460 389 X

Foreword

This year, the Young Writers' 'Poetry In Motion' competition proudly presents a showcase of the best poetic talent selected from over 40,000 up-and-coming writers nationwide.

Young Writers was established in 1991 to promote the reading and writing of poetry within schools and to the youth of today. Our books nurture and inspire confidence in the ability of young writers and provide a snapshot of poems written in schools and at home by budding poets of the future.

The thought effort, imagination and hard work put into each poem impressed us all and the task of selecting poems was a difficult but nevertheless enjoyable experience.

We hope you are as pleased as we are with the final selection and that you and your family continue to be entertained with *Poetry In Motion Lothian* for many years to come.

Contents

Leigh Gapinski (14)   80
Nicola Gill (15)   81
Jessica Wesley (14)   82
Kirstie Lingham (12)   83
Lewis Atkins (11)   84
Chelsey McQueen (11)   85
Jennifer Connelly (12)   86
Ashley Walls (12)   87

Dunbar Grammar School
Rachael Lees (12)   88
Amy E Thomson (12)   89
Stewart Robbie (12)   90
Megan McArthur (11)   91

Gracemount High School
Heather Thorburn (12)   92
Keith Rutherford (12)   93
Nicole Maloney (12)   94
Gemma Middlemass (13)   95
Sean Ward (13)   96
Nicola Anderson (13)   97
Jennifer Sime (12)   98
Ross Carruthers (12)   99

Lasswade High School Centre
Nicola Stalker (13)   100
Martha Gavan (13)   101

Merchiston Castle School
Edward McCaul (15)   102
Duncan Biggar (12)   103
Jamie McIntosh (12)   104
Alistair Reece (12)   105
Mike Oswald (13)   106
Farooq Javed (12)   107
Lewis Deaves (12)   108
Stuart Dalrymple (12)   109
David Thomson (12)   110
Brandon Kwok (13)   111

St Mary's Music School, Edinburgh

Whitburn Academy

Steven Allen (14)	151
Kirsty Boyd (14)	152
Sarah Macey (14)	153
Stacey Swan (14)	154
Ashleigh Campbell (13)	155
Teirnie Miller (14)	156
Stuart Wright (14)	157
Louise Hewitt (13)	158
Steven McCallum (13)	159
Garry McIntosh (14)	160
Lewis Macaulay (13)	161
Amy Stewart (14)	162
Nikki Sked (14)	163
Kelsey Henderson (13)	164
Gary McKenzie (14)	165

The Poems

The Gypsy

The embroidered clothes,
The silver threads,
The flowing skirts,
The coal-haired head.

The gold-ringed fingers,
The jangling feet,
The big brown eyes,
The tambourine beat.

The gathering crowds,
The wilder dances,
A puff of smoke,
The gypsy vanishes.

Erin Fulton (13)
Bo'ness Academy

Edinburgh Zoo

This is the place
Where the white rabbits are
And others with copper and ebony fur coats.
Can you please buy me? I am frightened.
Their eyes like beads
Also the horses clumping along the ground.
They are light brown, ebony and white.

The elephant is grey,
The elephant's body is as long as a limousine
And the monkeys jump
From tree to tree.

The pigs smell horrible.
They slump along the ground,
They are salmon pink
And they squeal.

Parrots are clever
And they put on their brilliant shows.

Vicki Stokes
Bo'ness Academy

The Bus Stop

Sitting at the bus stop
Waiting for a bus
Minding my own business
Not making a fuss.

Sitting all alone
Staring at the ground
I cannot hear a whisper
Not a single sound.

People staring out their windows
They must think that I'm dumb.
I'm waiting for my bus
But it still hasn't come.

So I started to walk home
It started to rain,
I was all alone
And I fell over a drain.

My vision was so cloudy
I couldn't really see
It got so bad
I didn't see the great big truck coming towards me.

The headlights blared
The driver honked his horn
He stuck his head out the window and yelled
'Get out my way you moron!'

Kirsty McKay (13)
Bo'ness Academy

Different Opinions

Why is there such a problem with the difference in age?
She says, 'It's only nine years you know!'
'We're in love,' she says!
'She's my baby girl and he's a man
How can she do this to me?
She doesn't understand, she's just a child!'

'It's only nine years,
We are in love!
I don't see the problem
She just doesn't want me to be happy
She hasn't even opened her eyes to see
All she can see is he's a man and I'm a child
How can she do this to me?
She doesn't understand! I'm not a child!'

'A man going out with my 13-year-old daughter!
No way, I'm not having it!
He's 22 you know
He's mucking about with her brain!
Why won't she listen?
She loves him more than she loves me!
I just want to protect her,
She's going to get hurt.
I'm going to kill him
How can she do this to me?
She doesn't understand she's just a child.'

'We're not doing anything wrong!
What's the problem?
It's only nine years.
I love her more than life!
God, they dictate to her, and run her life.
She has a spirit and they're killing it.
They're going to lose her
They don't understand
She's not a child.'

Stephanie Taylor (13)
Bo'ness Academy

Teamwork

As shocking lights
And banging noises
Struck around

With dead faces
And dead bodies
On the ground

In the army together
We were taught to stay

And the people that hadn't
Dead and cold they lay.

Bang! I felt a pain in my arm,
I hooted to my friend Greg
Who looked alarmed,
He fixed it up and here I was to stay.

Robert a rather independent man
I watched him across the field as he ran.

But now I know I am here for a real reason,
Because he got hit,
Like I got hit,
But now he ain't breathing.

Teamwork.

Jordan Thomson (14)
Bo'ness Academy

What Could You Spare?

People live in the world of yesterday,
We live in the world of tomorrow,
They cannot look forward,
We find it hard to look back,
What have they done to live like that?

No money, no food, no tools to grow it either.
No running water, not even a tap,
What have they done to live like that?

They don't want any handouts,
They just need a hand,
Please could you spare them about a grand!

Mark Armour
Bo'ness Academy

Leaders Are Weird

Do you need a leader
to tell you what to do?
Do you need a leader
to control your life?
Do you need a leader
to take you to war?
I need a leader,
this country needs a leader.

They might be slightly weird,
with their suits and briefcases.
They might be slightly weird
in their opinions.
They are all very weird
but we would be nothing without them.

Our Prime Minister has very funny hair,
it looks like someone has put a badger on his head.
He speaks very funny, all pompous and proper,
but what would we do without a comedian like him?

David Paton (13)
Bo'ness Academy

Our World

What happened to our world?
Is it the way we bring up each boy and girl?
So many problems in society.
Overcrowded towns and poverty.
Kids running amok with weapons
Creating an overpowering sound that deafens.
Shootings, suicide, murders too,
Are you sure it couldn't happen to me or you?
What happened to our world?

Daniel Snedden (14)
Bo'ness Academy

No Use

Fire alarms ringing in my ears,
raising everybody's fears,
but it doesn't here,
they go off all around the year.

Crowded hallways,
no room to move.
Litter everywhere,
but do they care?

Tin cans, crisp packets,
chewing gum on people's jackets,
sticky, awful, horrible mess,
the cleaners don't need a test.

One lone boy against a wall,
people around want him to fall.
Hitting, punching, verbal abuse,
are the teachers any use?

Written graffiti all around,
the culprits they won't be found.
What an environment
not exactly heaven sent.

This is meant to be a school,
I don't want to leave a fool.
Now you've heard what it's like
do you think I'm right?

Jenny Lynch (14)
Bo'ness Academy

Friendship

It comes, it goes
it can be there for life
the hurt, the happiness, the jealousy, it all shows
when the link falls
the pain cuts like a knife.

Friendship sits in the palm of your hand
it rises and falls just like the tide
it can sweep you away
or keep you standing
friendship comes and friendship goes!

Lori McLay (13)
Bo'ness Academy

Stamp Out Bullying

The crashing and thumping up against lockers!
It's the sound of children being bullied.
Thrown across the room, almost like a rag doll.

Why is it happening?
Something should be done.
Why's it not being dealt with.

The sound is deafening.
The teachers must intervene.
It must be stopped.

Graham Meikle (13)
Bo'ness Academy

Edinburgh Zoo

I went in a zoo,
animals around,
I couldn't hear the guides talking
because of the sounds.
Looking at the tigers
makes you curious,
you think a tiger would go for you
because it might be furious.
I saw a tiger pouncing up and down
it could pounce really high
in Bo'ness town.
It roars like a bear
and looks like fire,
I think tigers are better than bears
they jump even higher.

A snake in a cage
hissing to me,
I don't understand what it said
but it looks like it wants to be free.
Slimy little hissy snake
has eyes like beads,
it slithers for food
that's what it really needs.
They are the two animals
that I like in the zoo,
everyone would love to
come here, even you!

Nicole Nisbet (13)
Bo'ness Academy

Where Will They Lead Us?

They start the wars
and leave the public to finish it
Bush is just nuts
Blair is too scared to disagree
oil is running out
the Queen doesn't care
and Saddam is God knows where.

Arguments everywhere
with Chirac and Tony Blair
Americans killed more Brits
than anyone else.
Friendly fire . . .
there's no such thing.

Adam King (13)
Bo'ness Academy

Edinburgh Zoo

This is the bear that has fur like chocolate,
all round and fluffy. He roars like a tiger,
runs faster than humans,
has eyes like buttons
and feet like small stones.
He is surrounded with trees and water.

This is the penguin that looks like a boy wearing a suit,
small and thin.
He waddles and does not run.
Eyes like small beads and feet like baby shoes.
The penguins are surrounded by rocks and a pond.

This is the monkeys that swing through the trees
and screeches as it swings through the grass-green trees.
They are tall and thin with a tanned body
and with a tail that looks like rats.
Eyes like small buttons and feet like small baby hands.

Gillian Meikle (13)
Bo'ness Academy

Edinburgh Zoo

Snakes slithering along the ground
hissing because they are cage bound.
Its eyes cry out, 'Free me!'
A stroke of sorrow runs through me.
The parrots squeal in joy and laughter,
they fly and lie.
They look so happy flying there
I didn't want to leave
For there was no despair.

The fish squirm through the water
looking like blades chopping through wood.
The water splashes,
flying past but the fish stop at last.
At last I saw them go shooting past, into the window.
The olive green water came spewing out.
The fish struggle to get back.
People run to fix the glass
but they were too slow at last.

Dean Hunter (13)
Bo'ness Academy

Edinburgh Zoo

This is the place where the anaconda raps around the tree.
It slithers its funky tongue at me.
It's like a long winding road.
The owl is like a statue.
It has buttercup eyes.
I thought to myself this creature is wise.

Kai Bertram (13)
Bo'ness Academy

She

She stands alone, a living doll
Contemplating should she fall?
Her white dress soaked with red
The children laughing in her head
Thoughts of suicide and her pain
They slowly turn her insane
When they're here she hides away
When they're not their voices stay
She sits alone with lonely tears
The voices pollute the noises she hears
The children laughing in her head
She knows that someday she'll be death
Until that day she sits alone
Dreaming of days now gone
She now sits here waiting for death
No more sorrow, just one last breath.

Kayleigh Parris
Bo'ness Academy

Divided World

We have life and good healthcare,
They have dying and despair.
We have clean water and food aplenty,
They are thirsty, starving and empty.

Our country is wealthy, spending thousands on education,
Their country is so poor it cannot stop the mass starvation.
Our country has good housing and transport to get about,
Their country has homeless, poverty and drought.

We think we're hard done by but really life's great,
It would be their life we really would hate.
We all should be equal, it's really not fair,
But nobody helps them.
Do they not care?

Emma Davidson (14)
Bo'ness Academy

The Same As Me

If the world could open their eyes,
If they could look and see,
That deep down inside of them,
They are all the same as me.

The colour of our skin,
Our culture or background,
We are all the same
Despite the few differences,
In personality, race or name.

We should not discriminate,
Against black or white,
Against race or religion,
Against beliefs or thoughts,
Because these minor differences,
Do not change who we are,
We are people.

If we choose a sexuality,
Different from everybody else,
Does that make us a freak?
Does that make us a criminal?
Does it make us a traitor
Because we are not the same as everyone else?
We laugh because people are different
They laugh because all of us are the same.

Nicola Rhind Mullen (13)
Bo'ness Academy

Christmas

Santa Claus is coming,
He's working in his workshop,
Making loads of toys
For all the girls and boys.

The elves are working day and night,
Loading Santa's sleigh,
You'd better go to sleep,
For Santa's on his way.

Mum and Dad are putting up the mistletoe,
They're kissing as they go,
We're putting up the Christmas tree,
We're happy as can be.

The presents are all gathering,
Underneath the tree,
Now we all go carolling,
Singing merrily.

Mother's making mince pies,
While Santa flies,
I'm lying on my pillow,
Gazing out the window.

I thought I saw a glimpse,
Of someone fat and round,
Then I saw him in the chimney,
Floating to the ground.

Christmas Day has come,
Our stockings have been filled,
Look at Christmas dinner,
Yum! Yum! Yum!

Christmas Day, Christmas Day,
Snow is falling,
We're with the family,
Our friends are all calling.

Christmas Day has gone,
We're sitting by the fire,
We're keeping nice and cosy,
We're all feeling dozy.

Emma Aitken (13)
Bo'ness Academy

In Edinburgh Zoo

This is the place
Where the brown snakes of fear are,
Slithering around in the grass.
The fish, rainbows, swim around in their ponds
Eating other small fish,
And the maroon monkeys
Are swinging from tree to tree
In their forest-like home,
Now to the tigers,
Orange and white,
Prowling around, eating meat and sleeping,
The penguins waddling around in their icy area
Make me laugh.
Ha, ha, ha!
There are people who are cleaning
The crocodiles honking,
While the crocodiles are there,
And I think it is quite smart,
Hooray, hooray, hooray!

Shaun Rutherford
Bo'ness Academy

Message To The Leaders

You stand at the top, the head of the tree
You also stand and watch it fall
You stand up there and say that it's fine
But it's going downhill all the time
You think we are here to be dictated to
We don't want to follow you
But if we talk, twitch or breathe the wrong way
'Be quiet son,' you are prone to say
You're more into politics and less into humans
Because of this policy you've lost your touch
Running this world and ruling us people
You stand and say, 'This is too much'
The troublemakers of this world wreak havoc with ease
They make you, the leaders, bend to your knees
We have to fight to save our rights
But you stop us, not them with your verbal bites
Just to show you have some might
To keep your egos at ridiculous heights
You let our lives get constantly disturbed.
All the alarm is really absurd.
Your rules and laws are vague and hazy,
Because you, the leaders are totally crazy
And after this world runs the course you have set
Through the middle of the middle to the end of the end
The question and answer you give yourselves shall be
Who should have listened? It should have been me.
The lesson you will learn that day,
Is, 'You should give the small people a say'.

Terry Gould (14)
Bo'ness Academy

Sanctuary Unknown

As I sat up one night
You passed my door then out of sight
I walked to see where you had gone
Maybe see where you had tread
Not to feel the nightmare score
When I stood there by my door.

Some eyes but I didn't see
Were searching and stalking me
As I walked out from sanctuary
As I walked down that street.

As I walked down the shore unknown
The footsteps behind me trudged
I had no safety then to go
As I walked down the shore unknown.

The feeling that I do feel
Like rabbit to the wolf
As I race down the paths and streets
Footsteps follow still
And the voice I sometimes hear
In my head as I escaped
You'll never be free from my stare.

And now I've realised
Sanctuary is far from it
No safety is nearby
For the eyes still watch me
And wait for me to come
To let them do what they want
And dispose of flesh and bone
And this is what I realised
As I watched you go.

Lucy Rodger (15)
Bo'ness Academy

Amber Eyes

Amber eyes, shining brightly,
Gazing, emotionless into the flames,
Reflecting scenes of fire destroying,
Seeking revenge, burning hopes.

Amber eyes, full of hatred,
Staring, intensely, at charred emotions
And smouldering ruins,
Reflecting faces, filled with anger,
Showing no remorse.

Amber eyes, watch the gun,
Watch the trigger,

Bang!

Amber eyes, left to bleed,
Lifeless.

Alison Wevling (15)
Bo'ness Academy

The Lonely Old Man

A lonely old man,
Sits in his chair,
No one who knows him
Gives a care.

An old basset hound,
Lying up curled,
His only friend,
In his lonely world.

Living in poverty,
His life's a mess,
None of his friends,
Could care any less.

A tear-stained photo,
Of his late wife,
Is all that keeps him
Fighting for life.

The only thing
That keeps him sane,
Is his alcohol,
In his life of pain.

He's now feeling poorly,
Haggard and old,
Only wearing rags,
To keep out the cold.

He curls up tight,
On his chair in the street,
The hound is whining,
At his feet.

The world gets darker,
It's the end of his life,
He drifts to sleep,
Off to see his wife.

Nicola Maclean & Stacey Martin (12)
Bo'ness Academy

Alone

As I lie in my bed
I begin to wonder
Why my life
Is like rain and thunder.

The floods wash over
And take away
All my sunshine
And happy days.

What is the point?
Why am I here?
When all I do
Is shed my tears.

Ashley Furby (13)
Bo'ness Academy

The Wish

I wonder what it would be like
To be a spaceship in the night.
Up above with stars so bright
I wish I could, I think I might!

In my ship so shiny and new
Launch date near, lift-off due,
Countdown starting, nearly there
A great excitement in the air.

Above the Earth in the great black sky
I see the planets whizzing by,
Down below the human race
Great wonder and amazement on their face.

It was all so quick, gone in a flash
We enter Earth's atmosphere with a blast.
'Wake up, wake up!' I hear a voice say
It's my mum, oh bother, it's a Monday!

Lindsey Jackson (12)
Deans Community High School

Midnight

As I sit upon the rusting swing
Looking around the empty park
The pale moon bare
Luminous above the trees.
As I feel the bitter breeze across my face
And hearing the trees rustling
In the dark
All alone
As the clock strikes midnight
I leave, walking slowly towards the pitch-black road.

Catriona Tainsh (11)
Deans Community High School

Enter The Legend

Deadly as a bat,
Reactions of a cat,
Talented this man must be.

Eyes of a hawk,
Body like a rock,
Strong this man must be.

A disciplined man,
Could strike through a can,
But dead this man was to be.

Although he is gone,
His spirit lives on,
For he is . . . Bruce Lee.

Iain McClafferty (15)
Deans Community High School

In My Past

I sit in a dark room
Waiting for you
With one candle lit,
I shed a tear for you
I wait as the hours pass
You're not here now,
You're in my past.

Tammy Johnston (15)
Deans Community High School

Boys

Boys, boys,
They play with their toys.
Oh what the joy,
Of being a boy.

They eat like pigs
And they pretend they have wigs.
They behave really bad
And they drive you mad.

They say they are hard and tough,
But really they are silly and stuff.
They always forget their things,
And like Ali G they wear gold rings.

They always lose at games
And they forget people's names.
They say rude things now and again,
Oh boys, they really drive you insane.

I wonder how the girls cope,
And the way the boys hope.
Oh the joy
Of being a boy.

Kay McAdam (12)
Deans Community High School

Time Has Come

All on my own
all in the dark
fate cast in stone
light against black
time has come for me to let go
to pack all my things and get on with the show.

Hurting inside
not letting it go
it's too hard to hide
you already know
time has come for me to tell all
to get on with my life and answer your call.

Getting it out
head held high
never a doubt
that it would pass by
time has come for me to finish the line
letting you know that I'm doing fine.

Claire Reilly (13)
Deans Community High School

Shooting Star

I was looking at the stars,
twinkling away,
I saw something,
flying above my head
with a shine,
like a flashing light shining.
I quickly made a wish,
I went home,
I saw my wish standing there
waiting to give me a hug
in the past 3 years.

Lisa Chung (16)
Deans Community High School

Sounds Of The Sahara

The African sun is golden
As it casts shadows on the sand.
When it's level on the horizon
That's when the sun touches the land.

The grains of sand are warming
As they trickle between my toes.
My hair is gently moving
As the Saharan wind blows.

I travel on my desert ship
Upon the sandy sea.
The dunes go on forever
For all eternity.

The silence is deafening
As we move with the caravan.
Not a single noise is heard,
From camel, bird or man.

It's such a lovely feeling,
To see what I have seen
And all that I can say
Is I'm glad that I have been.

Robyn Mackenzie (15)
Deans Community High School

Darkness

Darkness
Is the emptiness within the soul
It stalks you
Like a tiger stalks its prey
And before you know it
You're overshadowed by this dark tiger
There is no escape
There is no hope.

This blanket of darkness
Follows you wherever you go
It dozes in the dusk
Waiting for the right moment
You escape this cold blanket
But you'll have to face it
Again and again
Forever.

Ashley Tait (14)
Deans Community High School

Terrorism

Why oh why did you let it happen?
Why didn't anyone stop it?
But on that day so far away,
No one could have imagined what was about to happen.

People were oblivious, getting on with their lives,
Whether that was a child walking to school, thinking of the day ahead,
Then suddenly, a gigantic noise fills the air and the sky is filled
                                                        with dust,
Coughing and spluttering, trying to find a place to hide,
'What is happening?' they ask.

Or whether that's a man just settling down to his work
                                    in a bank nearby,
Just getting on with his work, minding his own business,
Then, so out of the blue came an ear-bursting noise
From somewhere nearby then people start running for their lives,
What is happening? they wonder.

Then, like a smashed bullet, so many people were taken away,
And now because of that day, no one can really get on with their lives,
Everyone looking over their shoulders,
Listening to world leaders on the news,
But we all know that the world will never really be the same again,
Until the real terrorists are found!

Amber Murray (12)
Deans Community High School

War

War is such a strong word
War is not a kind word
War is a very harsh word

There is no reason for war
Problems can be solved

War kills
War hurts
War ruins
We make the people who lead us into war, *heroes!*

Heroes do not cause so much pain
Heroes do not cause so much damage
Heroes do not send innocent men to fight

We send our own men to fight
Miles away from their homes

The victims of war are innocent
The victims of war can't get on with everyday life
The victims of war are scared

War is not cool
War is not funny
There is no reason for war!

Natalie Anderson (12)
Deans Community High School

Sports

Gymnastics is the best
Better than the rest
Cheerleading is cool
Cause all the girls rule
Rugby I like
Even though I stink

Swimming is great
I always stay up late
Singing is fun
So is playing in the sun.

Nicole Walker (11)
Deans Community High School

Running

Running is something that you do
In situations running is helpful
But in others running is wrong

You can run from your fears
You can run from your friends
But you can never run from yourself

You can hide from your fears
You can hide from your friends
But you can never hide from yourself

You can talk to your friends
You can talk to your family
But it is not hard to talk and tell lies.

David Gilfillan (12)
Deans Community High School

Starry Night

The stars come out at night
Twinkling in the sky
Like tiny little diamonds
Shining up from high
And the shiny, yellow moon
Looks down on us below
Brightening up the sky with its friendly glow.

Shannon Gallagher (12)
Deans Community High School

A Gift

A gift from me to you
Something special, precious and true
Its eternity you cannot doubt
It will never wear out
To use up would be impossible
Nor, to digest, it's neither edible
Invisible you cannot sever
It will always last forever
To leave behind you wouldn't dare
It goes with you everywhere
A gift only I can give
With you every day you live
Something special, precious and true
I give my heart to you.

Leigha Henderson (12)
Deans Community High School

Canada

Your face is like a ray of sun
Your beauty blinds my eyes
When I'm with you it feels so rich, we're always having fun
I hate leaving you when I go home, saying those sad goodbyes.

I wish that I could stay closer to you
No more talking all night on the phone
If I lived closer it would be no more
Me and you we would be a pair, just us two
I'd stare into your beautiful green eyes thanking God I was not alone.

Finally our wedding day would come
I'd put the ring on your finger
After a year we would have our first son
My heart goes weak I begin to linger.

Lee Kane (16)
Deans Community High School

Scarred

From the scars upon my arms
Can't you see I'm hurting?
Feeling pain, shedding tears,
Can't you see I'm hurting?

I look in the mirror and see my face
Tear-stained and deserted
My eyes are welled up with tears
Crying for no reason.

Why am I doing it?
Why do I care?
It's eating up inside me
It'll always be there.

Gina Moir (12)
Deans Community High School

Wild Horse

A wild horse gallops through the night
A wild horse is never scared
A wild horse gives pride in his mare.

A wild horse's eyes gleam bright
His coat shimmers during the night
His heart rushes, his spirits are high
While he rears in the sky.

A wild horse stands in the night
His mare nearby, his filly in sight
They join the herd and gallop around
The sound of their hooves thundering on the ground.

He stamps his hoof and tosses his head
As he gives a loud neigh and the wild horses go to play
A wild horse gallops through the night.

Hayley McEwan
Deans Community High School

Why Did She Go?

A room with nothing in it,
A room with no light,
A room - no one in it,
Where has she gone?
Her life here has ended,
She's not with me,
She's off in her own world,
With friends and boys
And somewhere to go.
She's with me everywhere I go,
Right in my heart,
So everyone knows
That she is my sister
And I love her so.
But where did she go?
Why did she go?

Victoria Livingstone (14)
Deans Community High School

Box

I am trapped in a box,
Surrounded by people I don't like.
I feel out of control,
I want to disappear,
To a place where I am happy and free.
I am being pulled in so many directions.
Can't someone help me?
Can anyone hear me?
If you can hear me,
Help and get me out!

Samantha Dewar (15)
Deans Community High School

The New Boy

The new boy stood in a corner
And no one would go up to him.

He had never been seen before
And people were treating him like a new book.

Some boys next to me said he was stupid,
But I knew they were just judging him -
Like judging a book by its cover.

In class he never speaks, as he is like a locked diary.
He came from far away and he moved so much,
His life is like the chapters in a story.

A girl in my class said,
'He lives in my street and his parents are so strange,
They are like characters in a novel.'

He is so thin, he is like a page of a book.

I feel sorry for him - the new boy because I know how he felt,
After all, I was a new boy too.

Steven Stoneman (12)
Deans Community High School

Stereotyping Yourself

Line us up, just like slaves
Make us neat and pretty
Take away everything we have
And strip us of our pride
Kick us when we're down
Because we're just 'nobodies'
That you think you know . . .

Werner Nel (14)
Deans Community High School

Goldfish

It glides past without a care,
It has no worries, it has no fears.
Its orange scales shimmer in the light,
How beautiful it is.

It swims round its bowl, oblivious to the world's true form,
It sees the world through rose-coloured glasses.
It feels no harm, it has no boundaries.
It swims as far as it wants until it hits the glass.

One day on life's journey round the bowl,
A strange creature to the goldfish jumps beside it.
It has four legs and is black and white,
It seemed to be a peaceful creature.
Then suddenly the calm waters turn into a stormy sea,
As the creature plunges its leg into the bowl
And swipes it up and has it for dinner.

Jordan Lawson (12)
Deans Community High School

My Worst Nightmare

My worst nightmare is English homework
Essays and poems - I don't know where to start
In fact, I'd rather not do it at all
I would much rather be out riding with my friend
Or lying in my bed listening to my radio

I'm dyslexic and for me that means I'm slow at reading and writing
In fact my handwriting is so messy and my spelling is so bad
it is hard to read
English, closely followed by French are my worst nightmares
Somewhere in-between are science, maths, BIT and geography.

My favourite subjects are CDT, art and home economics
Lots of practical work which I enjoy
The right side of my brain which works the best
Gets a chance to plan, design and create
With the minimum of *reading* and *writing*.

Fraser Andrew (13)
Deans Community High School

Questions

People asking questions
Asking what is wrong with the world today?
Asking questions every day

As I get ready to go out
I look into the mirror and ask myself
What is wrong with the world today?

As I walk down the street
People all around me, I can see them asking each other
What is wrong with the world today?

As people meet for dinner
I see them looking at each other over menus asking
What is wrong with the world today?

As I get ready for bed
I look into the mirror and ask myself
What is wrong with the world today?

Natalie-Jane Cairns (13)
Deans Community High School

Dogs

Dogs are like humans
Man's best friend
Dogs come in all different breeds
Colours
Sizes
They are cute
Cuddly
Friendly too
Dogs are not toys
They are for life
Dogs are also playful
Caring
Intelligent sometimes
They might get sad
But most of the time their tail will wag
Collies are my favourite
Black and white is cool
I have a Collie
What about you?
Dogs can help people
Or do jobs to help
Police
Farmers
Blind people
Needy
Dogs are like humans
Mine is my best friend too.

Ashleigh Ballantyne (13)
Deans Community High School

War

They were all lined up,
Waiting for the fight.
Guns at the ready,
The enemy in sight.

They attacked in great force,
And at a fast pace.
They drew their guns and fired,
Soldiers falling in their place.

Guns, bombs and dying men,
Lives lost in such a haste.
The men remaining dropping like flies,
The lives lost are such a waste.

The way it goes no one can win,
The people weep for those who died,
Especially their kin.
The sad thing is that's how it goes,
Even more so,
That's what everyone knows.
The war has ended,
But that doesn't change the fact,
The families are filled with grief,
At the government's act.

Mark Wilson (13)
Deans Community High School

War

It carries on through days and nights,
It's far more serious than playground fights.
Sweat drips from people's faces,
Different people and different races.

Guns from trembling hands shot,
Piles of blood left to rot.

In the air bombs begin to fly,
People back home cry and cry.
How can people be so mean?
Such disasters which eyes have seen.

People at home anxiously wait,
Dreading to hear of their loved one's fate.

For some they will never know,
As the years go by,
And their children grow.

Katy Anderson (13)
Deans Community High School

Fear

Innocent people die and disappear,
Anger spreads with unmistakable fear.
People held captive all on their own,
Killed or arrested for making a groan.
Some strong people pride their hope,
People protest and pray to the Pope.
Men are arrested without any proof,
Houses are burned from floor to roof.
Any thread of hope is quickly wiped out,
No answers come forth so the questioners shout.
Walking around eyes on the ground,
Those who resist run or are found.
The torture rooms quickly fill,
The army are happy, they are licensed to kill.
The army have no heart, their blood is chilled,
For every smile possessed, two humans are killed.
No noticeable water for the poor to drink,
Your life is the price, for saving what you think.
The cycle of life is forcibly ending,
No help from those on whom they were depending.
The waiting is over, the hero has arrived,
To give you the world of which you've been deprived.
The fighting is over, it's been a bumpy ride,
If you look hard enough the hero's inside.

Blair Trotter (13)
Deans Community High School

Talking In Whispers

Why must it be like this?
Why can't I say what's on my mind?
Talking in whispers,
Moving in silence,
Too scared to talk or think.

People being tortured,
People being killed,
The house of laughter
Is filled with screams.

Although there is nothing I can do,
My dad's being tortured,
My mum's been killed
And I also suffer,
Suffer in silence.

I hope that one day peace will come
To all of my country,
One day it shall come.

Jennifer Marshall (12)
Deans Community High School

Why Does He Do It?

I wake up in the morning and the fear hits me like his fists,
I'm fine at school but the fear comes back when the teacher
                              shouts, 'Class dismissed.'

I walk slowly home all by myself, no friends to call my own,
But the only thing I worry about is stepping foot inside my home.

I open the door and there he is, as drunk as a man could be,
He smacks me and before I know it I'm down on my hands and knees.

My mother then falls beside me, with black rivers down her face,
Her mascara has run, her face is red, he calls her a disgrace.

My mum and me are worth more than this; we shouldn't have to
                              put up with his rage,
He's not even my real dad but he makes me feel like I'm in a cage.

I can't get in, I can't get out until he says I can,
Every day I try to think why my mum would marry this man.

But one day I came home and he wasn't there,
I was quite shocked, but I honestly didn't care.

My mum gave me a hug, then smiled at me, then told me to go
                              and pack,
Then we just drove away and I've never thought of looking back.

Now we live just the two of us, I have friends but only two or three,
But I don't care because for the first time we are happy
And for the first time we are free!

Michelle Sneddon (14)
Deans Community High School

War Poem

What do you know about war?
Is it the guns, the killing or maybe more?
War is not a game for young kids to play,
So, listen to what I have to say.
In war many people die
Because they are going to give
The future generation a chance
To live happily and give a glance
At how the soldiers saved them.

So what happened to the dead?
They lay on the battlefield and bled,
But their names will not be forgotten
As they lay in their old wooden coffin,
They are buried under a tree,
On their tombstones read RIP.

'So when he gets to Heaven,
To St Peter he will tell,
One more solider reporting Sir,
I've served my time in Hell.'

Ross Campbell (13)
Deans Community High School

Fight Of Life

People call him names,
Thinking it's fun and games.
He gets hurt inside,
He doesn't show it,
But we know it.

He has had to fight his way through life,
Wondering if the next time he fights it will involve a knife,
He can't fight this war against racism alone,
It's too hard,
He has had it tough,
Enough should be enough,
It's all said and done,
But he won't give up until he has won.

This is all because of his race,
Because of the colour of his face,
People don't believe he is the same,
But people like this have a name
And being racist is their game!

Allana Macdonald (13)
Deans Community High School

Why Not?

I felt a trickle run down my face,
As my heart beat at a rushing pace.
The whole world seemed to close in on me,
I thought this was the way life had to be.
Each night I'd lie awake in bed,
Not a word to be said,
I'd think and think about what to do,
Should I tell a teacher or should I tell you?

No one liked me, I don't know why,
All they did was make me cry,
Everyone in that crew,
They ripped my heart into two.
And for as long as I live,
Nothing will ever make me forgive.

Lesley-Anne Reid (14)
Deans Community High School

Ignorance

They crowd her
Surround her
Admiring her art.
The curves and colours flow in harmony
Slender, smooth like silk.
They have a desire to touch it
Grab it
Feel the beauty.
She doesn't mind, only takes it as a compliment
A little flattered
But thinks nothing of it.
Happy and cheerful she carries on
Creating a beauty that will live on.

Ignorance is bliss.

Colin Teevan (16)
Deans Community High School

The Foal

The little foal has reached his goal,
Of being born today.
The farmer's there to help the foal
And lays him on the hay.

As the farmer rubs the hay on the foal,
He takes a breath of air.
As the foal gets to his feet,
The farmer leaves the pair.

As the mum eats some food
And the foal drinks some milk,
They both feel safe and secure
In the barn that the farmer has built.

The farmer returns to take them out
And leads them out to the paddock.
The wife calls out to let him know
It is time to eat his haddock.

As the foal skips happily away
The farmer and his wife look out
And think, *what a happy day*.

After dinner the farmer comes out
To check on the newborn foal,
The farmer is shocked
To see he's escaped
Through a tiny little hole.

The farmer was worried and he hurried
Back home to get a flashlight.
It was very cold and very wet
And turning into night.

The farmer found the little foal safe
And fast asleep,
He was so very happy, he looked at his wife
And they both began to weep.

Rachel Elliot (12)
Deans Community High School

It Is The Wild

It is the wild that creeps
And crawls over land and sea.
In time never-ending
Over all things that be.

It is the wild that advances,
By all creatures' domains.
It will take its revenge
Till only sung legend remains.

It is the wild that remembers
When the world still was young.
The first whisper through the trees,
The moon on the mountain.

It is the wild that lives
In thoughts swift as fish.
This river ever steadily flows
To the world's simple wish.

Helen Gilbert (15)
Deans Community High School

You And Me

You think I'm different:
That's not true,
There's no difference between me and you.

You and me - we're the same,
I have a life,
I play the game.

I am human, just like you,
We're the same
Through and through.

I have dreams like I should,
I'd fly through space
If I could.

My family's always in fights:
Fighting for my people's rights.

I get home from school each day
And go straight back out
To earn some pay.

Our enemies think that we should change
But to me that just seems strange.

I one day hope to leave this space
And show myself with
Honour and grace.

No doubt I'll be teaching children of our way,
Hoping they'll help our enemy
Change one day.

In the future your kind will see
We're not different, you and me.

John Shearer (13)
Deans Community High School

War

People fighting, people dying,
Chemicals and gases filling
Lungs of little children,
Kids dying, some of the kids
Even becoming orphans,
There is something wrong
With the new world word,
War they say, it's to save
Thousands of lives,
At the end thousands die,
Some people even fight
Over money and oil.

Ibrahim Al-Nakib (12)
Deans Community High School

Death

A lonely hunter dressed in black,
Stalking everyone.
Its gaze pierces mud, trees, sky and even flesh.
You can never kill it, never capture it,
Never see it, never touch it,
But somehow you know it's there, watching you.
It will find you as it finds everyone,
It will never stop hunting.
It eats bone, skin, eyes and hair,
It will eat you whole.

Death, death, death! It's coming, it's coming
And when it does it's coming for *you!*

Cameron Clark (12)
Deans Community High School

Decisions

What are these things that rule our lives,
Which stab our minds like big sharp knives,
Turn our worlds upside down and tear us apart inside,
Making our hearts feel like the sea during high tide?
No, to make them is no easy mission -
Decisions, decisions, decisions.

Where do we go from here? What will we do?
Most of us - do we even have a clue?
Concerning matters of the heart, nothing seems clear,
Where do we start with things which seem so far, yet so near?
In our mind's eye we have all these grand visions -
Of making *decisions, decisions, decisions.*

Why is everything in life so difficult and hard to reach?
Maybe we should all start practising what we preach
And try to be sensible about our life's path
Or suffer from our soul's eternal wrath.
Between our hearts and our head, there is always a great collision.
Oh, *decisions, decisions, decisions.*

Hayley Pender (16)
Deans Community High School

Love

Why do people talk about love?
Is it in the dictionary?
What is it above?
Is it beside lost
Or maybe it's near cold?
Is it just a tale?
A story that's grown old?

Was love a miracle?
Will it only happen once?
Did it last for just one day
Or did it last for months?
Just two people found it,
But they never knew,
Love was not only just for them,
The word created grew.

Then it lost its passion,
The word which these two people gained.
The meaning for it lost,
But the word remained.
This word that people heard of,
They tried to do it too,
And create the meaning that was lost,
But we still don't know, by who?

Leeann Brown (17)
Deans Community High School

The Apple

A red sphere splashed with yellowed green,
Vibrant it glistens beneath a waxy sheen.
It gleams, it shines, light dances across its face,
It sits still and bright in its resting place.

Take up the apple, pick up the knife,
The apple recoils, fears for its life.
The apple struggles, cries in pain,
Tries to escape but all in vain.

Shimmering, voiceless the apple lies open,
The glimmering sphere now naked and broken.

Yasmin Alzadjally (16)
Deans Community High School

The End!

The end is close, the end is near,
For you and I, it all ends here.
The vague sun, the morning dew,
Memories of me, you have so few.
I am the birds circling in flight,
The stars so softly shine at night.
I am the wind that blows around,
The leaves that fall on autumn ground,
The moonlit beams, upon the trees.
I am the gentle midnight breeze,
The sky, the grass, the air you breathe,
Understand that this is me,
The end is close, the end is near,
For you and I, it all ends here.

Lisa Hunt (14)
Deans Community High School

My Lizard

I look at him, sleeping right there,
Off in a dream blissfully unaware,
His eyes are closed tight,
His face's an off-white,
Strange to think that to other males he is surly,
His tail's lying there, all nice and curly,
His legs folded back, he lies almost limp,
Hard to imagine him fighting, but he isn't a wimp,
What a wonderful creature sleeping so close to me,
He certainly is as happy as he can be.

Christopher Dickie (14)
Deans Community High School

Unjust War

Are we happy at the misfortune we cause?
All because we feel the need to dig in our claws.
We say that we're 'helping' them back on their feet,
But really, we want them to take a back seat.

Although it's their life, we want to take over,
Make ourselves wanted, whilst undercover,
The reason why they are in need
Is because we did a terrible deed.

Is this the way we want to live?
Knowing that the only reason that we give
Is because we hurt these people, more and more,
By causing an unjust and unfair war.

Fiona Brown (15)
Deans Community High School

The Midnight Mare

The midnight horse galloped into the sky,
The ground gave a shudder,
The wind gave a sigh.

Her dazzling eyes, her coat that shone bright,
She was the brightest star
In the darkest night.

She galloped through the undulating grass,
Through the trees
As the branches swept past.

She galloped up a cliff,
Just beyond the bay
And gave a most beautiful sounding neigh.

As the sea lapped gently on to the shore,
Onward she pranced
Until the moon shone no more.

The peace was shattered
By the crack of a whip,
With strong ropes around her
She was dragged aboard ship.

Destined as a work-horse, in a faraway place,
Up rose the wind,
The rain blew in her face.

The sea called out to her,
The men could not keep,
With a toss of heels
She plunged into the deep.

She swam for the land
As the sun shone bright,
She raced along the sand,
What a wonderful sight!

Heather Brown (12)
Deans Community High School

The Moon

Ellie went to the forest
And looked up at the sky,
'The moon can be so beautiful,'
She whispered with a sigh.

'Excuse me!' coughed a cricket
Who'd seen her earlier on,
'But sometimes when you're different
You just need a different song.

Listen to the swaying grass
And listen to the trees,
To me the sweetest music
Is those branches in the breeze.

So imagine that lovely moon
Is playing just for you,
Everything makes music
If you really want it to.'

Sidra Munir (12)
Deans Community High School

The Ocean

Tranquil or ferocious,
Icy cold or warm,
This place is where creatures roam,
Under the majestic waves of foam.

The symphony of colours varies very much
From blue, green or violet to aqua, silver, gold.
As the golden sunshine hits the rippling bay
The seals they clap and begin to play.

This place is called the ocean,
I wonder, did you know
That many secrets lie beneath
This place, full of wonderful things?

Stephanie Brown (12)
Deans Community High School

Any Regrets?

God gave us a world and expected no pay,
Then gave us the power to take it away.
He gave us a conscience and made us aware
And then it went downhill from there.
But whilst your lives you did 'enhance',
Nature didn't stand a chance.
But hey - that's their problem!
Don't listen to the 'eco-pests',
Go build your house on some birds' nests.
Don't stand in the way of change,
Or get animals out of the firing range.
Don't worry about chopping down trees,
Or dumping oil in the seven blue seas.
After all it's not your problem.
Now you stand and look back
And notice all the things we lack.
Too late now to admit we were wrong,
That won't bring back what's already gone.
So how do you prefer it - before or after?
Have you learnt from your misplaced laughter?
Still think it's not your problem?
Who can drink polluted water
Or breathe oxygen-less air?
Who can look at the skyline
And think it's better now?

Leanne Harper (16)
Deans Community High School

Me And Mum

'You will be the death of me,'
She said, anger rolling off her tongue,
'Can't you, won't you, don't you see,
You are never nice to me?'

'You always make me feel so mad,'
I said, rage exploding in my head.
'Can't you, won't you, don't you see,
You always make me feel so bad?'

'You never, ever talk to me,'
She said, fury basking in her breath.
'Can't you, won't you, don't you see,
You will be the death of me?'

'When we fight I feel so sad,'
I said, the rage now flowing out my head.
'Can't you, won't you, don't you see,
You are very special to me?'

Hazel Turnbull (14)
Deans Community High School

My Friend

It's so not fair my friend has gone,
The agony I feel is just so strong.
I think about her every day,
And all the things she used to say.
I can't believe we had to part,
But good memories of her will stay in my heart.
A thought that helps me deal with the pain,
Is that I know one day I'll see her again.
Nobody knows how I miss and love,
My friend who's with the angels above.

Lauren Sharp (14)
Deans Community High School

Leeway (Freedom)

A deep blue colour mixed with green,
A place where you have never been.
As I enter and break the surface,
I begin to forget this whole purpose.
I've gone and left this world behind,
Created one inside my mind.
Free to express my feelings, my thoughts,
With lots of colours, swirls and dots.
This place would be just for me,
The place I call beneath the sea.

Leigh Gapinski (14)
Deans Community High School

Never Again You

You hurt me every time but I come back,
Think I grow stronger but you prove me weak.
Life is full of holes, though you filled the crack,
My stomach turns every time that you speak.
I was lost in your world of dreams and lies,
I just wish I had noticed the sign.
To me you were perfect with no goodbyes,
Escape? No! I followed the party line.
Found someone new, though still lies temptation,
Don't want to go back, I am happy here.
Decision needed, not contemplation,
A place that's easy to rest all my fears.
Clear of you my feelings are not false but true,
it's him that I love, never again you!

Nicola Gill (15)
Deans Community High School

Mist

The mist clouded the toy-like city,
Swirling around, gobbling the buildings,
It mysteriously moves around,
Having no place to go.

It snatches light,
Leaving dark alone.
The ships can't come or go,
The planes can't leave with their passengers.

The mist takes over
And leaves nothing alone.
Suddenly the mist leaves,
Light, life, happiness all return!

The mist moves on to another city,
It has no home
So it causes chaos,
But leaves on its own!

Jessica Wesley (14)
Deans Community High School

War

The cannons fire, the bullets fly
To bring at dawn a blood-red sky.
The guns awake and strike open fire
To kill and demolish is all they desire.

The innocent men on the battleground
Wait, listening, there is no sound
Until the silence is pierced by the bullets, loud and clear
And for some, it is the last thing they hear.

Many die, few survive
With this killer that seems to thrive
On the blood of young children, women and men.
When will this war come to an end?

How many people will have to die
Before they end the fight and let it lie?
And for the loss of someone, who suffers more
Than their family and friends, whose hearts are torn?

War - it pierces the heart like a thousand knives
And it will keep on taking many more lives.

Kirstie Lingham (12)
Deans Community High School

The Moon

You can see the moon almost every night
High in the sky, grey and bright,
Covered in craters and scars.
It looks down at a blue world
Teeming with life in a black sky,
Waiting and hoping
That one day sometime soon
It will be visited again by
Its admiring neighbours,
Until then it waits and watches alone.

Lewis Atkins (11)
Deans Community High School

The Moon

Moon, moon you are so round,
They say no face to be found.
But every night you smile at me,
It's been happening since I was three.
Moon, moon come out to play,
Please, please don't hide away.

You are so bright up there in the sky,
There is nothing like you there in the sky.
It makes me smile each time you pass
Because I think we had a past.

I've grown up now, I am twelve,
But now you are just the moon itself.
I now know you have no face,
You're just that moon that hangs in space.

Chelsey McQueen (11)
Deans Community High School

The Beach

As I stood on the beach
With the sand between my toes,
Watching the waves of water
Going to and fro.

I could feel the warmth of the sun
And the taste of the salt on my lips
As I watched in the distance
The sails of the tall ships.

Soon the waves were lapping my toes
And the sun was begging to drop
As I stood there dreaming quietly
Wishing this holiday didn't have to stop.

Jennifer Connelly (12)
Deans Community High School

A Beach

A beach is a place where you can go and relax.
You can hear the sound of the waves hitting the rocks
And water and hear your feet crumble across the sand
With every footstep you take.

I can see the top of buildings far away
And the lighthouse is lit up.
I can see the water, rocks and lots of shells and little stones
And best of all the sand.

I can taste the salt from the sea breeze
And find when you swallow you can taste sand.

I can feel the sand tickle my fingers and toes.
I can feel the stones rub against my feet when walking to the water
And when you step in the water it is a shock because the water is cold,
Then you feel the wet sand on your feet.

You can smell the salt in the air,
The seaweed and the fish smell.

Ashley Walls (12)
Deans Community High School

Friendship

Friendship is like the blossom from the trees
Blowing through the wind,
Flying through the morning sky
The wind singing like a lullaby,
Birds singing in the trees
Harmonies sound like a lovely breeze,
The sun shining in the sky
I hope this does not mean goodbye.

Rachael Lees (12)
Dunbar Grammar School

Life

We take life for granted,
But when what we have is gone
We realise that it means more
Than just greed and money,
It means love and peace.
War will enslave us all
Whereas peace will set us free,
Your life is in your own hands.

Amy E Thomson (12)
Dunbar Grammar School

Anger

My anger is like red-hot chillies,
Ten times bigger than anyone's anger.
My anger is like soup that burns your tongue,
As hot as lava and as deadly as snake venom.
My anger is like a dragon that never sleeps,
As fast as a cheetah always ready to pounce.
Beware of me and my anger,
We are very dangerous.

Stewart Robbie (12)
Dunbar Grammar School

Happiness

Happiness is a bright summer sun, yellow,
It tastes like freshly picked strawberries,
It smells like a sunlit pine forest,
It looks like a paradise with a hidden waterfall,
It feels like the best feeling
Running through your body from head to toe.

Megan McArthur (11)
Dunbar Grammar School

The Rusty Old Fishing Boat

The rusty red fishing boat
Sitting by the sea,
The water goes splash, splash
All over the two poor sweaty fishermen.
The fishermen shivering
In the cold, damp freezing rain,
Drinking hot chocolate
And a wee chocolate biscuit,
The boat was rocking
Back and forward,
The miserable smell penetrates,
Fish slapping against the boat,
Seals roaring loudly and clearly,
The wind howling,
Then it gets louder and louder.

Heather Thorburn (12)
Gracemount High School

The Lonely Fisherman

One huge ocean for one fisherman
In a boat red and yellow,
Waves splashing against.

One night coming into shore
Waves get rougher by the minute,
Knocking him off course,
Running back and forward.

Anchor fails to hold,
Hours of waiting ahead,
A wife weeps at home.

At harbour she spots a jacket
Floating amongst the seaweed
And still the anchor will not hold.

The fisherman woke to see how far he had travelled,
He starts up his engine
But the waves start up again.

But then he puts his engine to full power,
The rocking of the waves send him running
Forward and backwards,
He splits his head open on the mast,
Blood running down his neck
But still he tries to get back, then he notices land,
Tooting his horn to tell everyone he is coming,
The tears turn to tears of joy.

Keith Rutherford (12)
Gracemount High School

Sail The Seas

The beauty of the calm seas howling in the wind,
The bubbles reach the top of the shore as the fish flap
Their exotic tails through the ripples of the water.
How wonderful it is to sail the seas,
The beauty lies beneath these mirror reflections
That shine into eyes like a lantern in the dark,
Our hearts will sail with the wind like a tall ship
On its journey to a faraway land.
Sail the seas, just sail the seas.

Nicole Maloney (12)
Gracemount High School

Sailors Sailing On The Sea!

Sailors on the sea,
Drinking some tea,
Killing fish as they sail by,
Smelling the smell of seaweed
On the old rusty boat.

Wind through the ropes,
Clouds sailing by,
Boat gently rocks like a crib
Through the night,
On the old rusty boat.

Typical unshaven fishermen
With sweaty clothes on having a laugh
As some are moaning in the cold
With tobacco in their mouths heaving nets,
On the old rusty boat.

Gemma Middlemass (13)
Gracemount High School

The Storm

Crashing water,
Chugging red boat,
Cabin brew spills,
Captain panics.

Storm gets worse,
Signal of lighthouse,
Seals and fish slip off the boat,
Sailors put life jackets on.

The boat starts crashing off the rocks,
Terrified sailors take cover in cabin,
Then the storm calms down,
The water is still.

Many sailors could have died of a heart attack,
Moving through the sea sailors celebrate,
Misty waters take us home,
Mooring. Home.

Sean Ward (13)
Gracemount High School

The Big Rusty Red Boat

Hear the sea roar as you go out in the big rusty red boat,
Smelling the sea makes you sick.
The birds go down and catch their prey,
Seeing all the bubbles the fish make.
Let down the net, catch lots of fish,
Seaweed comes up while the fish are flapping their fins.
The sea is like a mirror,
It can't go inside out or upside down.
The sea is just like a baby's blanket,
A long sheet of blue!

Nicola Anderson (13)
Gracemount High School

Cycle

Rusty red fishing boat
Lying in the sea,
Freezing cold fishermen
Waiting for a hot cup of tea.

Sweaty men pulling in the nets,
Fish slapping on the deck,
Men waiting on the spot
For night to come so they can stop.

Night has come and sea is calm,
Only light is the moon,
Fast asleep, tucked in tight,
The fishing men say goodnight.

Time has come to start again,
Up at 5 and back at 10
And they are all on the boat again.

The rusty red boat,
The fishermen at sea,
The rusty old wreck.

Jennifer Sime (12)
Gracemount High School

The Innocent Fish

I am a fish in the sea and the net is near,
These ropes are the things that cause my fear,
The people who catch us are like killing machines,
They are all mean and very unclean.
These people are killers, they'll eat us for tea
But the worst thing about them is they'll eat me.

So here I am waiting and praying
And all around me the waves are swaying.
Is this my time, am I caught
And at the market will I be bought?
So this can't be it, that's my bet
Unless I get caught in the horrible net.

Will I be caught or will I not?
That's all there is to be thought.
Am I finished? That's what I ask,
But for the savages that's no task.
The net is in the water, it's swirling around,
Oh no, it's getting near my ground.
The net's beside me, am I caught
Or not?

Oh no, I'm caught in the net,
It's not fair, my life can't be over yet.
As quick as a flash they pull me in,
My tail is caught and so is my fin.
They'll cut me up to a wee bit fish,
They'll serve me up in a tasty wee dish.
So that's me caught, my life was swell,
So as the sailors would say, fair-the-well.

Ross Carruthers (12)
Gracemount High School

Christmas

Christmas Day is a lot of fun,
In the snow and in the sun.
When it snows, what a sight,
Glimmering and dazzling in the light.
Some presents are big and some are small,
I'm not bored, no not at all.
On Christmas Eve, what a sight to see,
All the presents under the tree.
Christmas Day is a lot of fun,
We have presents for everyone.

Up at five in the morning,
Kids screaming and shouting and running around,
Opening the presents that put us in debt,
The PlayStations, televisions, bikes, games, games, games.
The car won't start because of the snow,
Going out to see the family, oh!
Preparing the Christmas dinner for the whole family,
The turkey, the gravy, the vegetables.
Ah! I wish, I wish, I wish.

Nicola Stalker (13)
Lasswade High School Centre

The Presence

Its presence is the thing
I fear the most.
It haunts my steps,
My dreams,
My thoughts.
I don't know what it is
Or why it stalks me
But it does.
Even to the park
With its peeling paint
And concrete ground;
The see-saw creaks
Up and down
Although no one is on it.
A breeze whips up,
Autumn leaves spiral towards me.
I quicken my pace, my senses magnify.
I'm sure I can feel its presence,
Can smell it,
Can hear his rough breathing.
I break into a run.
in my head I see it clearly,
See its mouth shape the words,
it dies to speak.
I run out the park
And see its evil smile,
And dangerous glint in its eye.
I hear the footsteps behind me.
I turn around, and see
Me.

Martha Gavan (13)
Lasswade High School Centre

Questions

What if I had done that?
If I had chosen differently,
If I had gone down that route,
A new path to a new place.

Where am I in this life?
Is this a pinnacle?
Is this just the start?
When will I find my place?

Where am I going?
Onwards and upwards,
Or am I destined for mediocrity?
Will I fly or fall?

When is this?
Is this a time of change?
A time of mistrust, war?
Is time even there?

What am I?
Just another heartless person?
Someone with no future?
A nobody?

What do I want?
Riches and luxuries
Or happiness?
Will I find neither?

Questions needing to be answered,
Answers needing to be found,
Will I find them,
Or will they find me?

Edward McCaul (15)
Merchiston Castle School

Black Labrador

The wet-coated, slobby Labrador
Lies beside the fire,
Outstretched like a carpet,
The wind and rain howling through
Cracks under the door,
But he was warm and snug,
Dozing in the limelight,
Out cold.

Duncan Biggar (12)
Merchiston Castle School

The Squirrel

Scuffling along from tree to tree,
Seems as graceful as can be.
There it was in mid-air,
Trying to gnaw that juicy pear.

Its acrobatic body flies through the air,
I'm telling no lies.
This rodent creature is only 1 pound,
15 inches long and 2 from the ground.

I am a squirrel,
You've probably guessed.
Afraid of nothing, I am the best.

I'm only a squirrel.

Jamie McIntosh (12)
Merchiston Castle School

The Invisible Jaguar

As I am walking through the jungle
Looking for prey,
Why do they fear me?
I make them pray.

From tree to tree I jump
Chasing monkeys all around, there they are
On the ground, I run
Still chasing, but too late!

Finally, there in the open a deer,
Getting closer and closer, until
I pounce, the chase is on,
Crack as the neck breaks, I am the best!

Alistair Reece (12)
Merchiston Castle School

The Otter

As it swims through the water
With its silky fur reflecting
The sun, it searches for food.
It swims so gracefully it looks
As though it was doing acrobatics
Underwater.

Then . . . it sees its prey and like
A homing torpedo it shoots after it,
Never losing sight of its target.

And finally *slam* go the otter's jaws
And its teeth sink deep into the fish's body.
Then, with its food, the otter leaves,
Leaving only a trail of *blood!*

Mike Oswald (13)
Merchiston Castle School

The Falcon

The falcon is the boldest bird of prey,
The fastest and meanest
Of all the birds of prey.
When the falcon sees its prey
It will use its speed to
Dive towards the target
With no worries of missing,
it grabs the prey from the back
And pulls it back to the nest
To feed its young.

Farooq Javed (12)
Merchiston Castle School

Monkeys

I am a monkey swinging in the trees
But of course I don't swim in the dangerous blue seas.

I don't wear pyjamas but I do eat bananas
And I am as brown as a Twix.

I have big long legs but a very small head
And I also have very big arms.

I never go down to the ground
Because I might just be a little bit too loud.

And even though we are in a bunch
The snake could still eat us in one big munch.

I am also reasonably fast
But I still can't get past.

The two-eyed slithery snake
That can kill me like a rake.

Lewis Deaves (12)
Merchiston Castle School

Squirrel

There is a movement in the leaves,
Then a scuffling in the leaves,
There is a commotion up the tree,
The gleaming eyes of the red squirrel stares,
Takes a moment and runs further up till it's hidden.
When all is quiet the climber comes down,
Its hands are full of goods.
It makes a wave-like movement in the leaves,
Then it stops,
But then it puts its head above the leaves,
Head down,
Then runs for the tree,
But then there is no return.

Stuart Dalrymple (12)
Merchiston Castle School

Cheetah

Dangerous and deadly, he steals through the night
Quiet as a mouse, spotted coat bright.
Quick and swift goes the mighty cat through the dark, gloomy night,
Flying past at the speed of light.

Then with his back legs high he shifts into gear
And as he goes past animals they cower in fear.
Now the warning is out: the cheetah is here,
Birds fly through the air knowing that the fast cheetah is near.

It finally happens - the cheetah has struck,
It has taken the life of a wandering duck.
Now his day has come to a close
But the cheetah will be back to break some more bones.

David Thomson (12)
Merchiston Castle School

The Dolphins

Dolphins, dolphins with their smiling face,
Swimming at their fastest pace.
Rising out of the sparkling waves,
Always with their happy face.

Happy is the way dolphins look,
Happy is the feeling that dolphins took.
They make you happy and never sad
And they will always be your friends.

In and out of the water
They always try to jump higher,
When next time they jump again,
They will say, 'Will you be my friend?'

Brandon Kwok (13)
Merchiston Castle School

The Daily Fox

Foxy, Foxy of the day,
Down underground in the dark and gloomy den.
Sleepy, sleepy snore,
Off to bed . . . 'Aaahhh,' snore, snore.
Foxy, Foxy of the night,
Out in the cold and darkness of the night.
Sniff, sniff here and there,
Slap, bang, pounce, tear, tear.
Some food for the young cubs,
Some food for Mum
And most of all some food for *me!*

Grant Walker (12)
Merchiston Castle School

Siberian Tiger

The Siberian tiger,
Ruler of the ever icy, cold Siberia.
Its pure, clean, white fur coat and its jet-black stripes
Make a perfect disguise in the white woodland.
Its strong, powerful paw with its four sharp flick knife-like claws.
Its mouth, packed with long, razor-sharp teeth,
Flanked with powerful jaw muscles
Which all adds up to a perfect kill,
The work of a professional, clean and cool.

Ross Barbour (11)
Merchiston Castle School

Panda

Black and white
I lose my eyesight.
There are five pandas
Crawling under the sun,
Eating leaves like a chocolate bun.

Black and white,
It is dark and bright.
There are three pandas
Snoring on the grass,
Sounds like the instrument brass.

Black and white
They run to my right.
There is one panda
Staring at my face
And finally I walk away.

Tom Chow (12)
Merchiston Castle School

The Cat

He slowly creeps through the long grass
Making not a sound,
His prey in sight,

Slowly sneaking up on it
Then pouncing.

It struggles hard
And tries to run away
But does not escape.

The mouse, was not lucky,
This time.

Eyes glistening, well fed,
The hunter of the night departs
Into the trees beside the long grass.

Craig Nunn (11)
Merchiston Castle School

Wolf

Wicked teeth glinting in sun,
If I had a choice to move, to run,
I'd disappear, I'd be gone,
I would get away.

Howling to a moonlit sky
We humans used to wonder why,
One wolf howls but not attacks
Just in a group we call a pack,
To cut, to kill, to slash, to bite,
Sharp enough to kill the type
Of people that would shoot them,
The type of people that would abuse them.

The wolf packs are not sinners,
Though they take no prisoners,
Unless to them they're kind,
The weak are left behind,
The weak are left to die,
They only attack if provoked,
One swift bite to the throat
Ends all at nightfall.
The wolf . . .

Rory Fairweather (11)
Merchiston Castle School

The Hamster

Down the hole,
In the ground,
Lays a stash of food.

In the corner
Is the sound
Of the golden hamster.

Lettuce, seeds and nuts
Is what
He is storing.

In the night
The hamster is
Being very cautious.

The predators
Of the hamster
Are wide awake.

The hamster
Is spotted
And is being chased.

Weaving in and out
The plants,
He is running.

He jumps
Towards his hole
Hoping to escape.

Down, down
Into his hole
He scampers.

And he is
Safe.

Scott Warden (11)
Merchiston Castle School

The Cat

Long, sleek, elegant, ferocious,
This is the way of the cat.
He prowls through the garden silently
As he approaches the dark bushes
Where the small brown mouse scuttles across the grass.
Pounce, he glides,
Landing accurately on the spot where the mouse sits,
He digs his sharp teeth into his prey,
Then silently walks away.

Isa Sher (11)
Merchiston Castle School

Midges

Midges, midges come out to play
when the evening sun has gone away.

Round and round these fiends do fly
sucking at your blood supply.

On every Scottish camping ground
these annoying insects can be found.

They bite and bite and make you mad
and altogether it makes you sad.

The only way to be content
is to run and hide inside the tent.

And stay there hiding all the night
until the morning's welcome light.

Duncan Nicholls (11)
Merchiston Castle School

Squirrels

When all the squirrels wake up
And start to jump the trees,
They're having fun until one falls,
He falls and then he's dead.

All of the other squirrels cry
And then they bury him,
So all the squirrels stop and pray for him.

The next minute the squirrels forget
And start to have more fun,
And when its bedtime they stop and pray for him.

Kyle Smith (11)
Merchiston Castle School

The Chessboard

The never-ending battle between good and evil,
Into battle, the valiant knights ride,
A skirmish takes place between the armies,
The bishop appears,
The light in the dark, the moon in the night,
Then, the queen, supreme being of the battlefield,
Moves here and there,
Before the slow charge of the pawns, before death,
The queen glimmers one last time before she joins the rest,
The end is near,
Checkmate.

Rory Williams (12)
Merchiston Castle School

The Ninja

In peaceful and happy
Feudal age Japan,
The Ninja, fast as a bullet,
Swift as the wind,
Leaping as high as the trees,
Defies the laws of gravity.
Balances on the cherry blossoms,
For all eternity.

Jake Maxwell (12)
Merchiston Castle School

Sonnet

I stand on the bridge while waiting in the dark
And then the shadow appears from the mist.
Instead of nightingale, I hear the lark.
Then I saw you and knew we should have kissed.
Rain falling down, upon my thinking head.
I wanted you to leave, right then, but no.
My life will never be the same - you're dead.
I see your face in everything I do.
How will I begin to live life again?
I need you, miss you, long for you each day.
I try each day but still my heart feels pain.
'Be strong my love, I'm with you all the way.'
But life goes on, fond memories of love,
I'll see you up in Heaven with the dove.

Oliver James Hairs (12)
Merchiston Castle School

Dad Ironing

It was in the morning like a battle-cry,
The king of the clan rages war through noon,
With the ironing. On, on he goes until the afternoon,
Will he do it by tomorrow?
He cannot lie in, it drives him crazy,
As he tries to iron the bedsheet.
Worn out and defeated, he goes to sleep,
But his happy dreams turn
To nightmares,
As the bedsheet and iron go strolling down Elm Street.

Alastair Valpy (12)
Merchiston Castle School

Getting Out Of Bed

It all begins with the sound of your alarm,
You lie motionless without a care in the world,
You are king of your room and don't want to leave,
Then all of a sudden the lights go on
As if you have attempted to escape from a prison.

After fighting a battle against sleep
You climb the long way down out of your bed,
You are slapped by the cold winter air
And realise that you forgot to close your window.

You walk what seems like miles
Over to the bathroom where you slip
Slowly into the tiny room which is your shower,
You push the water button
And you are blasted into awareness.

Ross Lumsden (14)
Merchiston Castle School

Hoovering

You chain the huge sucking beast to the wall
And let it run wild around the room,
Terrorising the local residents
And destroying the peaceful environment.

From room to room it glides around
Feverishly sucking everything it can get,
Occasionally coughing up fur balls
And chewing on old dusty rugs.

Just as it threatens to rip up the carpet
It emits a loud terrifying sound,
The beast falls silent and sits there
In docile fashion, waiting to be unchained.

Then, with a pat on the back,
It makes its way back to the cupboard.

Tim Rennie (13)
Merchiston Castle School

What Am I?

As the darkness overcomes the house,
Everyone falls silent.
Then suddenly, we move, like soldiers,
Taking food dropped from the humans.
The door opens again,
We stop like well drilled machines.
A human enters, taking a jacket from the wardrobe
And then leaves.
As the door closes,
We start working again.
We work day and night,
We work hard and fast,
We work in groups.
So much going on,
That humans don't know about.

What am I?
I am an ant.

Billy Kwok (14)
Merchiston Castle School

The Choir Of Durham

It was dark and snowy,
The towers of Durham loomed up high,
There were lights in the cathedral flickering and dancing,
They lit up the stained glass windows.
It was cold,
A slight sound of music could be heard,
It came to me only as dreamy harmonies.

I entered the cathedral,
The iron-studded door creaked,
The atmosphere was welcoming.
Music flowed and drifted through the lofty space,
The beauty of the building was echoed in the music,
A wooden carving of the baby Jesus seemed to cry.

I sat and got lost in the airy spaces,
The music seemed to swallow me up like water,
The only light was from candles,
They lit up the faces of the angelic choir,
It brought memories,
Tears flooded into my eyes.

I remembered singing with the choir,
My emotions stopped,
Durham fell silent,
The music had stopped.

Ben Goulter (13)
Merchiston Castle School

Nature

The house overlooks a metallic-blue sky,
With boats swaying calmly in the morning breeze,
A speedboat scuttles across the sheet of glass
Causing ripples to roll up on to the island.

The tranquil garden is sheltered by waving trees,
With shades of sun gaping through the bare branches,
A lone rabbit darts through the dew,
Killing the stillness of my peaceful hideaway.

In the sky is a sphere of a yellow glow,
Putting a twinkle in the water's eye,
The cool fresh air delights the robins
As they hop from branch to branch tweeting.

There is a line of smooth hills stretching the horizon
With poppies forming a red rose blanket,
Everyone is out, using the world's creations,
Enjoying what Mother Nature has given.

Ruaridh Macfarlane (13)
Merchiston Castle School

Friend Or Foe

The wind was dulled
The sky was an odd grey
I could feel anger creeping up my spine
Like a spider crawling up a steel pole

I could feel the blood in my head boiling
Like a pit of red-hot lava
I could sense the poison of annoyance
In my veins
Pumping around my body like black blood

I had thrown him a lifeline
But he had covered it in filth, then thrown it back
Rejection had given me a solemn feeling in my stomach

His comment had given me the impression he had spat poison
I had made a tackle
And had been kicked off
Like I meant nothing

My heart was thumping
Giving me the impression someone was hitting me on the back
I had been sent off
The mud was splattering on my face
And it was raining by now
High tackle, there was no high tackle

My friend had acted like I had just hit him
I walked off in silence
No words could redeem what my friend had just done
The pain was devastatingly sore
I ran, ran in honour, I was never going to stop!

Chris Reid (13)
Merchiston Castle School

The Orinoco

Blue skies
Lush greens,
The odd site of civilisation,
Jungle!

Nobody around other than the natives.
They try to sell you items,
You can't resist,
You would buy anything.

The murky water,
The line of bubbles rising to the surface,
From catfish at the bottom,
You can't see them as it's so murky.

Later on you eat one,
The delicate texture enters your mouth,
You cry for more.
You could eat bucket-loads.

You enter the green vegetation, wanting to explore,
Finding out more about the people,
How they live,
What they hunt.

You swim in the water,
You can't see your feet,
When you get out the guide tells you what you swam with,
Piranha, dolphins, giant otters, electric eels and more.

You slept in a hut in the middle of nowhere.
You fished and swam with piranha, you even ate them,
You trekked in the jungle with wild jaguars.
You've been to the Orinoco.

Cameron Johnston
Merchiston Castle School

School Dungeon

The rain attacked our heads from above,
As we went to our next class.
The teacher's eyes hit me like daggers,
I had forgotten homework,
Again.
I soon found myself in detention,
The walls compressed me.
The teacher's shadow loomed over me like a demon.
My pen felt like a lead weight,
The paper, drying cement.
My back was getting scars from the 'demon's' glare.
All drops of sunlight had faded out of this solitary cell of doom.
Would I ever escape?
Escape, the word was appealing, almost appetising
As I smelled the 'demon's' brew!
Would I go insane or was I already?
Hmm, not quite.
My hand ached and I felt the teacher's enjoyment
As I writhed through this torment.
Argh, a ray of sun hit me like a bullet out of a gun.
I was free, as the teacher lurched away.
I had won this battle.

Mark McCann (13)
Merchiston Castle School

The King Of The Wood

It starts a feeble sapling,
Swaying gently in the wind.
Vulnerable. Prone to death.
Slowly it inches bigger,
Growing its muscle and might.

Year after year it watches,
Sprouting healthy green buds in spring,
Abandoning them lifelessly in autumn.
Brown, orange, tinted wastepaper.
In winter its branches go ice-cold.
Hard, black silhouettes against a harsh winter sky.
Still its icy bark holds out.

Summer sees the tree bathed in light.
Soft, warm, shady.
Its broad leaves mottle the skin of the earth below.
The tree swaying in the light breeze.
Ever growing.

Soon it towers above its forest colleagues.
Years have become days, hours, seconds.
It whispers its tale to anyone who passes.
Singing in a choir of wind and leaves,
Crescending and diminishing from day to day.

The tree collects many sovereign rings.
It stands tall among its fellow competitors.
Will it ever be toppled from its high throne?
This most noble king of the wood.

Charlie King (13)
Merchiston Castle School

Lambs To The Slaughter

'Captain's here *now!*'
The shriek of the referee
Shatters my fragile thoughts,
And around it lingers the vile air
Of a patronising snob.
Unwilling to leave my nervous team,
I trudge warily through the mud-scarred terrain,
My heart pumping boiling liquid around my body,
That leaves me feeling numb and senseless.

The enemy is awesome,
Bulging with body mass,
Like weak dams with water,
Set to unleash sheer power and terror.
Their captain marches forward,
Professional, experienced, prepared.
To him, I think, I am no leader.
I call heads, it says tails.
The milky mist glues itself in place.
The charge forward draws nearer.

Back I run, to reunite with my teammates
'Into positions! Positions!'
As one they react to my orders,
Like an iron fist.
'Tail gunners ready!'
The referee strides into the centre.
A sombre silence spreads over everyone,
Like an infectious disease.

I glance proudly at my team,
Wearing their uniforms with honour.
Awaiting the first wave of the enemy attack.
The wailing whistle stabs at the thick air.
My men charge forward as one,
Like missiles freshly released,
But also like lambs to the slaughter.

Leo Collins (13)
Merchiston Castle School

My First Trip On A Plane

We boarded the plane,
My father and I.
It was a big, monstrous beast
With a skin of metal and blood, oil.

We sat in our seats,
I looked around.
There were lots of people,
Old, young, screaming babies
And people with uniform.

I was looking out the window,
Suddenly the ground began to move.
Moving forwards.
The plane was moving!
Then the lights dimmed.

'This is your captain speaking . . .'
I wasn't listening,
It was getting dark outside.
Two long rows of lights stretched out into the distance,
The plane turned.

There was silence.
Then the engines roared into life.
The deafening noise penetrating the thick hide of the beast.
The plane lunged forward
And gathered speed.

The nose began to rise,
Then the fuselage followed,
Higher and higher,
Faster and faster,
My first trip on a plane.

Thomas Handley (14)
Merchiston Castle School

My Great Day

It was a cold, wet
and windy day.
And I was doing the most
stupid thing imaginable -
playing in a rugby tournament.

Despite the awful weather
there were a lot of spectators,
who came to watch a
rugby tournament
in the middle of nowhere.

It was my first tournament
as a captain.
In the first game I was
very, very nervous,
but this soon wore off.

Everybody played well because
you had to move so
that you wouldn't freeze to death.
Because of this we
won our games.

As I went up to collect
the trophy, the rain splattered
into my face.
We had won the tournament.
The feeling was of absolute grace!

Bruce Mustard (13)
Merchiston Castle School

Night Down In The Backyard

It was a silent, chilly night,
Lights faded away behind my back,
As I entered into a piece of absolute darkness,
I could feel an ice-breeze sweeping past my face,
I walked down the deserted path,
With two black bags held in my hand,
Time drifted so slowly,
As if I'd been left alone in this place for hours,
An unidentified moving object shot past the corner of my eye,
I felt my heart beating so hard,
As if it was going to beat out from my chest,
I took a deep breath,
Trying to wash out the fear in my mind,
I carried on on my unknown journey to the skip,
With fear and images cascading through my mind . . .

Rickie Cheung (14)
Merchiston Castle School

The Camp Of Hell

We arrive. A sudden rush of anxiety rushes through my body.
I'm shaking, shivering, butterflies flutter inside.
For no reason I'm worrying.
Who knows what about?

I arrive.
As soon as I set foot on that campsite I feel left out.
I've been here 2 seconds and I want to leave.
I start to resent my mum and dad for sending me here.

I'm all alone in my sleeping bag, wide awake.
Not saying a word.
Everyone else is having fun.
I'm not.

Minging food greets me in the morning.
I need the toilet.
The toilets are so smelly a pig wouldn't feel at home,
I have to hold it in.

I even felt left out doing the activities.
'Pass!' I call.
'How about no?' they reply.
I cry inside, my heart begins to ache.

A week's passed, I'm starving.
The sight of my mum soothed my heart.
'I'm leaving!' I cry with glee.

Alasdair Abram (13)
Merchiston Castle School

Whales

The magical, majestic creatures
Slide into the waves of the sea,
As the white foam swallows them up
Into the bottom of the sea.

The whales using the tiniest bone
In their tremendous body
To make divine tail rise up
And then down to the seabed.

Then another follows the same move
Until there are four all following
The same carefully choreographed spectacle
Until they are gone.

Where did they go?
Your mind tells you to
Think things totally absurd
As you try desperately to
Bring back the amazing creatures.

Then up they come, one then another
Full after their gigantic feast
Their stomachs splitting at the seams
From the tonnes of food.

Then they are gone!
All of them gliding into
The vast world of the sea
Their home!

Anthony Dale (13)
Merchiston Castle School

The Storm

The gold sphere rises in the blue-grey sky,
A ray of light flashes, awakening the Earth to another day.
The wind blows little more than a gust,
Nothing moves,
The day has risen.

There is a faint sound of birds singing far away,
The gentle flow of water seeps in-between rocks and stones,
Trees stand still, lost in time, unable to move,
Then, a crash of thunder.

The gold sphere is covered by a thick, grey cloud,
The light is hidden and the Earth covered in darkness,
A sharp gust of wind blows, picks up leaves from their resting place.
Rain lashes down and in seconds the trickle turns into a fast-flowing
stream.

In seconds it is all over,
But the vicious storm has left its mark on the land.
The birds that once sung have returned to the warmth and
        shelter of their nest,

The land cries a cry that no one hears,
Then the silence is once more
Only to be awoken by the mighty sphere.

George Campbell (13)
Merchiston Castle School

My Brother

He is my greatest friend.
He is my greatest enemy.
He is my very foundation.
He is my demolition crew.
He can make me laugh.
He can make me cry.
He can make me dance.
He can make me stand and watch.
His words can be soft.
His words can be harsh.
He can be relaxed.
He can be stressed.
He can be calm.
He can be quick to anger.
I can love him.
I can hate him.
He can love me.
He can hate me.
I can choose to help him.
I can choose not to help him.
I can choose to be there for him.
I can choose not to be there for him.
He is unique.

I would have no one else in the world.

Struan Fairweather (13)
Merchiston Castle School

A New Day

Dawn's lingering breath drifts
Lazily over the dew-stained blades of grass,
Turquoise in their elegance
As they waft noiselessly from side to side
In timeless dance.

The birds glide silently through the cool, crisp air
As the sun's silken rays begin to immerse the land,
Like a handkerchief falling to the ground.
A musky smell hangs motionless and heavy,
Waiting to be dispersed by the warmth.

Swaying rhythmically in the gentle breeze,
Leaves rustle on branches laden with pale blossom,
Their subtle fragrance mingling
With the balmy mood of early morning
Before they float
Gracefully, twirling in slow motion,
To carpet the ground below in soft petals.

The cotton wool clouds majestically crown
A sky painted in shades of sapphire,
And deep below the glistening greens of the forest canopy
Life begins to stir and a new day is born.

Jonathan Gemmell (13)
Merchiston Castle School

My Special Place

My special place is wonderful, relaxing
And very peaceful. It's never too far away.
Sometimes you can be so absorbed you fall asleep.

It lets you visualise your wildest dreams.
You can see things more beautiful
Than a thousand green flashes
But my special place doesn't cost money
Yet it is priceless.

Some say you can't survive without it
But some can survive.
But you can ignore something you desire so much.
My special place is not unique.
In fact it is one of many.

My special place is not a secret.
Every night can be a different adventure
From pirates to a teddy bear picnic
My special place is my bed.

Gregor Morris (13)
Merchiston Castle School

Shot

The light fades into nothing,
A deep purple takes its place,
My time is now.

The engine roars into silent vibrations,
The lights flash on and a grim face is revealed,
A metallic clink as a fatal weapon is prepared,
Its slim body amplifying the darkness around it,
Off we roar, silently, waiting for the time to come.

A thin mist hangs lingering,
A protective shield,
Shapes lurk in black mobs of high grass,
Slowly we creep, noisy silence,
Our prey unaroused.

Beside me a light flicks on,
Its strong beam gleams like a single predator,
Still it searches, unfolding black landscapes as it goes,
A shape moves and the predator is on it,
We wait, poised like a spring,
A chance, a hesitation is all it took,
I whip my companion's slender arm round,
My finger tenses,
One squeeze was all it took for a latch to unlock,
A steel python to speed forward,
A single shot to fly through the air and find its target.

The creature lies dead,
Blood trickles out of it like wine to toast my first shot.

Angus Sinclair (13)
Merchiston Castle School

Frame Of Your Past

So sturdy, upright
Holding on tight
Glitter and gleam
Plain or sheen

Any shape
Any size
Cut my insides up
Work with me

Holding colour
Holding light
Perhaps a candle burning bright
Or a bird in flight

Time will pass
But alas
I'll stay
Until I'm put away

Which not for a while
I'm no trial
Just a frame
Of your past.

Laurie Anderson (15)
St Mary's Music School, Edinburgh

The Last Hour

Quiet
Small rustling and bumps
Space
Then all noise at once

Quiet again
Compressing heat and light
Sun
Comes streaming in to strike

Emptiness
Minds wander and wish
Movement
From the hands of the
            numbered dish

Time
Is far off and
Freedom
Grows nearer, darker grows his twin.

Soon
We feel it coming, slowly
Gradually
Throats turn dry . . .

Growing
Is the sun, piercing eyes
Growing
Is the heat, numbing the mind

Bang
It is here, all disappears
Swish
It is a memory, as evening nears.

Jonathan Rendell (15)
St Mary's Music School, Edinburgh

The Synonym Snake

Have you ever seen the synonym snake,
his skin and eyes both blue?
If you yank his slimy tail,
he'll speak in synonyms to you!

'A synonym is the same as a cinnamin,
a cinnamin the same as a leaf.
The leaf is the same as an ostrich egg,
that being the same as green beef.'

I laughed and I chuckled, I grinned with glee
as I listened to silly snake's song.
As more and more people came around,
we danced in a merry big throng.

'A toilet's the same as a tea kettle,
a tea kettle's the same as a tin.
The tin is the same as a chocolate bar,
that being the same as a bin.'

Then all of a sudden a bright and old man
came along and corrected us all.
He told us what a true synonym was -
a ball is the same as a ball.

And then the fun stopped, the little old man
had taken away all our glee.
Then one by one we all walked away,
very glum and very sadly.

I think the snake is still around, though none of us
have seen him for quite a long while.
But then again, reports have said
he's been spotted in the street of North Gyle.

Have you ever seen the synonym snake,
his skin and eyes both blue?
If you yank his slimy tail,
he'll speak in synonyms to you.

Peter Innes (12)
St Mary's Music School, Edinburgh

City Jungle

The wind moans like a plague child,
Cars screech like a dying man,
Street lights stare like hungry predators,
Rain trickles down buildings like freshly-drawn blood,
Bright diamond stars grip to the sky like claws into flesh,
Shop doorways creak like an old man's bones,
Car engines whisper to each other secretively,
The dark black road slithers like an angry snake,
Stray cats crawl as if they hadn't been fed for days,
The moonlight gleams over the dark, ominous city,
An old man shuffles, poking in and out of dustbins,
Then disappears on his own into the shimmering, silver moon.

Emily Ferrie (12)
St Mary's Music School, Edinburgh

The Giant

Hailstones lashed down
Rattling nearby buckets
And knocking on doors
Playing tricks like little boys

The tarmac road screeched in agony
As the cackling cars gouged scars in it
Stones crumbled beneath the mighty giant's feet
Its glaring stare split into a sneering grin

It turned
The hail had changed to snow
The giant pounced into the watching beam of a nearby streetlight
Onto the first flake of snow

The shadow was gone
The giant was diminished
It was a cat
It was gone!

Rosha Fitzhowle (12)
St Mary's Music School, Edinburgh

City Jungle

Rain lashes across the rooftops
Lightning flashes across the heavens
The wind roars like the jungle's lion
And rattles the windows in the town

Towering houses moan
And open their jaws to scream
Smoke bellows out the chimneys
Shrill screeches come from within

Muffled laughs come from the distance
Dustbins tumble down the street
Drooping flowers cry for shelter
As floods of rain pour down on them

Taxis creep around like spiders
Snakes slither round the bend
Motorbikes roar like thunder
Hedgehogs brave the speedy cars

As I crawl up in a corner
I can hear my mum's voice near
Then I wake up - it's the morning
And find out it was just a dream!

Jennifer Sterling (12)
St Mary's Music School, Edinburgh

Darkness

What is darkness?
Is it white-less
Or is it a shadow
Being cast by the meadow?

People say it is a figure of the mind,
But the people who said that were blind,
So what is it?
Is it somewhere we can visit?

So many questions,
But not very many answers,
The dictionary says it is the absence of light,
But what about during flight?

In a plane you can see there is a lot more,
Than our world to explore,
So when light is absent,
Where does it come from?

So you think this is a mystery,
Well there is a lot more for our discovery,
You humans are useless,
For if you can't understand something,
You call it 'unknown'.

But I know what it is,
It is senseless!
Humans just try to make sense of it,
Just like you are doing now!

After reading this you will try to make sense of it,
But that is in your nature, everyone does it!

Steven Allen (14)
Whitburn Academy

Baby

I open my eyes for the first time
I see ugly faces staring down on me
Language being spoken
But none of it making sense

Getting passed from body to body
Being examined in every way
Being spoken to but can't reply
I just cry

I go for walks
Though I don't know why
I sit in the buggy
Looking at the sky

This woman looks down on me
Handing me toys
Trying to get me to sleep
I am not tired

Finally I give in
What a day I've had
Toys, walks, being passed like a doll
I shut my eyes
I slowly drift off into a deep sleep.

Kirsty Boyd (14)
Whitburn Academy

Friends

Sometimes they make you laugh,
Sometimes they make you cry,
Some things that they do,
Make you want to curl up and die.

But when I'm feeling down,
When I'm feeling low,
To her is the first place I will go,
Because she's my best friend,
And I'll never let her go.

Sarah Macey (14)
Whitburn Academy

Love

Love doesn't require open eyes,
But instead an open heart,
For eyes are sometimes blind,
To what the heart sees from the start.
Love doesn't need to make sense,
Or even be understood,
Love isn't always meant to be,
Even though you think it should.
Love is sometimes magic,
But magic is sometimes fake,
Love is made of decisions,
And risks you have to take.
Love exists in your memories,
Love is always in the back of your mind,
Love is something that is lucky to have,
And something that is very hard to find.

Stacey Swan (14)
Whitburn Academy

Laughing!

Laughing is contagious
Something you hear every day
No matter what mood you're in
It always brings a smile to your day
Even when you're lonely, sad or whatever the mood
Laughing will always be around you
So when you're down in the dumps, laugh and smile
And your black cloud will disappear!

Ashleigh Campbell (13)
Whitburn Academy

The Kulling Fields

I feel fuzzy, what's going on?
Can't open my eyes, I can't see.
Feels like I've just been born,
Is that what's happening to me?

The rocky shore, the cooling ocean,
My flippers hurt but I press on.
My mother sets us both in motion,
The waves begin to keep me warm.

Fish flee before us, but it's time for tea,
They make a tasty meal.
It's great being able to swim in the sea,
I love my life, being a seal.

A peaceful day just lazing around,
A noise in the distance, I can't be bothered.
Then I hear thuds on the ground,
I turn around to ask my mother.

I turned to face her, terror in her eyes,
'What's going on?' I squealed in fear.
I looked behind me, another surprise,
Men with blades were drawing near.

One grabbed me hard by the head,
I called for help, he didn't understand.
Ignoring my cries, he raised his arm instead,
A large pointed razor held in his hand.

I looked at my mother, her body lay still,
What filled the air, a horrid sound.
Looking at the bodies made me feel ill,
Then I saw the blade come down . . . down . . . down . . .

Teirnie Miller (14)
Whitburn Academy

Music

Music is addictive
When you hear the beat,
Your body moves,
As well as your feet.

Music can put you in other worlds,
When you start,
To spin and twirl,
Music is addictive.

Stuart Wright (14)
Whitburn Academy

Heartache

What's the point in having a heart
When all they get is broken?
People like to treat them like
They're just a small token.
They use them
Then they lose them
And nobody cares,
Except us with the broken hearts, we care.
We suffer the pain
When the heartbreaker seems to have personal gain.
Oh there it is, I feel it again,
Just another heartache!

Louise Hewitt (13)
Whitburn Academy

My Mum

Oh my mum, she made my day
By giving birth she got me playin'
I was really good, a striker tae
When I was seven I played my first game
It was warm, it was grey
A very mixed weather day
We won the game, I scored a goal
After the game, she bought me a ball
My mum, she supported well
'Cause if we lost she lost a war
She wanted to keep me happy
I was as well, but if we lost I wasn't at all
I got so good I was a professional
I played for Man United
Yes, I was the star, every fan's idol
I signed a deal, the transfer went through
As I left United for Madrid
I stepped onto the Bernabeu
I sniffed the grass
It smelt so good
I stood on it with my brand new boots
The air in Spain, it smells so much sweeter
Even better when I beat the keeper
Madrid, we won the league title
Even won in the Champions League Final
My mum, she died so I retired
Without my mum I had no support
I left something I loved because I lost the other
Makes me think where I would be
In football without my mother.

Steven McCallum (13)
Whitburn Academy

The Babe

When I saw the girl at hockey
I thought she was so mint
I didn't try to act that cocky
I was trying to drop a hint

I played against her, hurt my arm
Then she brought my stick back over
She was such a gorgeous babe
I thought I had found a four-leafed clover

There were other lassies in her team
But none as hot as her
I pointed her out to Jason
He really did concur

I told the rest of the team
Barry knew her best
He didn't really fancy her
Unlike all the rest

She played defence, I played attack
Not much else can be said
I stayed stationary most of the time
And just stared at this gorgeous babe

You should have seen the way she looked at me
I knew she liked me too
Don't despair - the next time I see her
I'll know what to do

This tournament is annual
I want to go next time
She must have been that damn hot
For me to make up this rhyme.

Garry McIntosh (14)
Whitburn Academy

The Battle

This day was upon us
We had to win
I got to the stadium, nodded my head
And made a grin

I entered the changing room
Everyone looked up
The spirits raised
Already they thought they'd won the cup

We kicked off
All guns blazing
Five minutes had gone
We were playing amazing

This wasn't a game
It was a battle
We went into fifth gear
Pushing at full throttle

Play died down
They began to attack
Just like the soldiers
In Southern Iraq

The heads went down
We thought the game had gone afar
But two seconds later
I hit the bar

I followed it in
And hit a shot
Before I knew it I'd scored a goal
Two games on the trot

That game for us
Was our claim to fame
Not for the other team,
They hung their heads in shame.

Lewis Macaulay (13)
Whitburn Academy

Poems

Christmas
Light, crisp snow falling,
Chestnuts roasting on the fire,
Exchanging bright gifts.

Autumn
Leaves changing colour,
Weather turning bitter cold,
Crunching through crisp leaves.

Hallowe'en
Glowing of pumpkins,
Changing your identity,
A time to be scared!

Amy Stewart (14)
Whitburn Academy

A Bad Mood

When you're scared and lonely
And nobody is there
It will be a hard time for you
As nobody will care

Life seems so worthless
Not worth living anymore
Your heart feels like its dying
It's agony . . . so sore

But today is different
Everything is good
My friends and family support me
I'm no longer in a mood

My life is now brighter
Full of fun and games
I'm out my mood for good now
I'm so glad everything is the same.

Nikki Sked (14)
Whitburn Academy

Animal Cruelty

Helpless animals feeling pain
People protest but it happens again
They ask for help, they bark and yelp
There is no excuse, the animals are helpless
They can't really stop the abuse.

Kelsey Henderson (13)
Whitburn Academy

Football

The only thing I love to do
Is play football and watch it too.
My favourite player is Mark de Vries
He scores goals any time you please
I play football up the park
Pretending I'm my idol Mark
I watch hearts play in the Wheatfield stand.

I see people from all over Scotland
We play in Europe as well
A little different from Partick or Motherwell
I support my country, Scotland, always
I just love football and will all my days.

Gary McKenzie (14)
Whitburn Academy